T0063037

BURY ME NAKED

2022 © Teamhw SbonguJesu
All rights reserved

ISBN 978-0-620-97494-3
ebook ISBN 978-0-620-97496-7

Published by TNG Publishing
"TNG – The New Generation"
Pietermaritzburg, South Africa
TNGpublishing@protonmail.com

Distribution in Southern Africa:
TNG Publishing
TNGpublishing@protonmail.com

International and ebook distribution:
African Books Collective
www.africanbookscollective.com

Earlier versions of some poems were published in *New Coin*.

Grateful thanks to The Angel Network Durban.

Cover photograph: Teamhw SbonguJesu
Cover and text design: Scarlett Hartzenberg, Gugu Mtumane, Liz Gowans
Editor: Robert Berold

Bury Me Naked
Teamhw SbonguJesu

TNG PUBLISHING

Contents

III

IV

In memory of
Simo Simon Mhlongo
1964–2018

I

The beginning

It happened in October 1995.
Behind in rent
by a month or three;
my father, the beast, kept demanding
that mother pays her rent.
Drunk, in October,
his imprecise compliments were
for the first time
greeted with a smile.
He demanded to be let in;
for the first time, she let him in.
When inside he, again, demanded to be let in.
She again let him in.
He slept there.

A few weeks pass;
she tells him she's pregnant.
He doesn't want to believe it.
This would be his tenth.
But he could not kick her out,
he knew her situation:
she was 25,
this was her fourth,
she didn't have a job.
I was born.

Shortly after,
she fell pregnant again.
My father was not the father.
He kicked all of us out.

I opened my eyes for the first time when I was five;
I had five siblings,
all of us living with our mother
in a one room house at Imbali unit 13.

That exact day I met the father who impregnated her.
He was on top of her,
in front of all six of us—
knowing we were only pretending to be asleep.

They just threw me here

I am a result of two people's
uncontrollable libidos.
A 'wait' could have prevented it all.
Instead they went for it
raw, throwing me here,
in the deepest waters—
telling me nothing,
absolutely nothing.

They did not tell me I had to paddle with my legs,
and move my hands in a certain motion to stay afloat.
They didn't tell me how to hold breath when deep under,
and how to use my mouth when up.
They just threw me here,
expecting me to see for myself
like they saw for themselves.
Now nothing can be taken back
or undone.

Now all I can do is fold my arms
and sink.
And sink.
Hoping the ground is nearer.
Hoping my case will soon be done,
like theirs got done.

Exactly like them

I would see my mother
smoking something through her nose
and I would think
Never will you see me doing that.
I would see my grandmother and uncle
drinking together.
I would think
Never will you see me doing that.

Upon their deaths,
I went to live with my father.
A heavy smoker and drinker.
I would listen to him coughing
in the toilet and in his room
every single day and think
Never will you see me doing that.

I would watch him closely
when he was drunk.
He would struggle to walk, talk,
or even open his zip.
I would watch him start unnecessary fights,
being laughed at,
wasting money he didn't have.
I would watch him forget his name,
my name, our surname, every name.
I would watch him fall in love with women
who I knew he wouldn't have fallen for sober.
Sometimes I would watch him beating them up,
throwing their belongings outside our yard.
Never will you see me doing that
I would say to myself, angrily.

As my father and I grew older,
our personalities changed places.
By then I had done all the things
I said I'd Never do.
But still, I would look at my father
and say
Never will you see me doing that.

He changed.
He stopped drinking completely.
Got rid of all his friends.
Took no female (on earth) seriously.
Started hating everyone and keeping them at a distance.
He never took a big risk again, or any risk.
He never got involved in other people's problems,
no matter how minor they were or how much time he had.

Now I sit here thinking,
that so many of those Nevers I've already done,
and I don't see a reason not to do the rest

My father is back

I have these dreams
where my father is back.
Where he's moving around the house,
putting back things I have dismantled,
sorting out what I have forgotten to sort out.
Where he gives an ear
to everything I have to say.

I tell him about a girl I love
who'll never love me back,
about a close friend I now doubt,
and as I tell him, my problems vanish;
my muscles and joints, guts, chest,
brain and heart calm down.

When it's time to wake, however,
burdens and strifes stare me down
from all sides of my bed:
debts, hunger, threats,
and diseases—
reminding me I am an orphan,
and there's bending and sweating
to be done, before I can get
another chance to sleep and dream.

The funerals

I remember my mother's,
my two sisters',
my best friend's,
my father's.
Like it was yesterday.
Like it was today.

I can still feel their last presence,
I can still see their closed eyes,
and the forced expressions
that the corpse cleaners put on their faces
to hide their indifference.

I remember everything,
and God knows that's enough
to prepare me for mine.

Who gets what

Who should get the house,
who should get the car,
the furniture,
the clothes,
the gun.
How much will the lawyers take,
how much did the funeral cost,
how much has the executor misused,
how much is the taxman's share,
how much will be left?
Isn't the Master's office too slow? Hah?
Everything is being spoken about,
except the person who slaved for it all.

God silence

I don't want visitors,
they will see me struggle with my God silence.
They will see me wrestle with Him,
sometimes down, sometimes up.
Sometimes running away
from myself and Him. Sometimes hiding
at the corner of my imagination,
my face facing the wall.

I don't want friends,
they make me forget my God silence.
They open my mouth
and I become a gaping crocodile.
The bastards laugh hard at my light jokes
and nod and add comments—
I swim in oceans of false compliments.

I don't want a lover,
she will want me
to love her more than my God silence.
I will burst and break
into a million pieces
trying to please both of them.

I don't want anyone in my family,
they always want to show me their god,
or worse, remind me of what he can do
My God lives in the vague state,
and that's where I want to be.

They hate my God.
They say He doesn't answer,
'He is silent'.
True, He is silence,
He never answers.

Playing house

When I was young
there was a beautiful girl—
she was light-skinned, taller than me,
and was my neighbour.

One morning
my big brother and his friends were playing house.
The beautiful girl and her friends were called
and I was asked to join in.

When we began mentioning roles,
I heard her say she will be the mother.
I was the first to say I will be the father.
She changed her mind and said she will be an aunt.
I changed my mind as well and said I will be the uncle.
Her mood changed – she told everyone she will no longer play.
When asked what was the problem
her finger pointed at me.

My things were packed for me
and I was told to go home.
Everyone helped.

I went home and looked at myself in the mirror
for a long time,
trying to ascertain what was wrong with me.
I couldn't see anything—
my eyes were full of tears.

II

Bury me naked

When I am dead,
bury me naked,
facing the opposite direction
of the correct direction—
with my coffin and eyes wide open.

Throw the dust straight in my face,
use stones and bricks while at it.

When half done,
throw rubbish,
take a shit,
point your penises and vaginas,
pee and spit inside—
like you did on me and my name.

When done, leave.
Don't put any headstone,
or try to make it decent.
People should know
and not know who it belongs to.
Let them take a wild guess.
That shouldn't be a problem—
they are familiar with making guesses.

The deepest high
(Listening to M. Rabanye's Volume 1 at volume 60)

I have been pointed with a gun three times,
all three times I did the pointing.

I have been mostly lied to by my fears
and my long imagination.

I have died eight deaths.
The ninth is on the way.
All eight times I did both the killing and the burying.

I once tried to hang myself,
tied a rope to my room's roof.
But the thought of my neighbours' laughter
did not allow me to kick the chair.

When it was time to stand up and be counted,
I lay down and chose to be counted out.

I have been pointed with a gun three times,
and all three times I was a coward.

Handcuff all the angels

Handcuff all the angels
and torture them however you want.
Send them to get back all the blessings
they have unfairly distributed.
Dethrone God.
Throw Him in jail,
and don't allow Him any visitors.
Starve Him.
Hang His son Christ.
Not His portraits, rosaries or sculptures.
But Him.
Hang Him again,
and put all the nails,
not in His hands, but in His neck.
Hang Him from the ceiling of the highest darkest cloud.
Baptise Him with boiling chemicals.
Pour petrol and paraffin on the floor of heaven,
set it alight,
let there be no difference between hell and heaven.
No time shall be wasted reading any scriptures,
or kneeling or closing one's eyes.
Fighting and running is all there shall be time for.

There's more to life

My girlfriend is lying
next to me, dead drunk.
We have made love three times
since we arrived in my room
in the middle of this cold night.

On all three occasions
she didn't react to me being inside her.
Didn't wake up,
didn't move,
didn't make a sound—
except snoring
and clenching her teeth.

Tomorrow I know, however,
she will remind me of everything,
and thank me with a kiss on my forehead.

I never know exactly what she thanks me for.
Whether it's for providing her
with food and late-night accommodation,
or for the sweating I do during the night.

Nights like these remind me of
my English teacher back in school
who used to stare at me for a long time
and thereafter tell the class 'There's more to life
than sex, drugs and partying.'
I always wanted to ask him:
'Like what?'

My people

Where are the mentally unstable,
the drunkards,
the prostitutes,
the perverts of all kinds,
the thieves,
the murderers?
Where are the socially unacceptable,
the socially inept?

Take me there.
Where they are is where I belong.
I also want my insanity to change the world.

No one is bothered

My room used to belong to my father,
now it belongs to me, and my two friends.
We smoke in it,
drink in it,
host massive parties,
and fuck all different kinds of women in it.

As I speak, there are three 20-packs
of cigarettes on top of the coffee table,
six empty Broncleer cough syrup bottles,
three two-litre Sprite cold drinks,
a pack of mylan alprazolam pills,
and ganja.
A lot of ganja.

There's also
an empty litre of Smirnoff,
boxes of beer, filled tots,
overflowing ashtrays, dirty cocaine straws,
and a lot of snacks – we call them wash-down.

A skinny girl is in a room next door with my friend.
I know her, intensely, but I was not impressed by her,
so I gave her to my friend.
No questions asked, no condoms used.

We know nothing good will come of us,
and that we'll die young.
But we're not bothered.

My bed

It used to belong to my father, now it belongs to me.
It used to be soft, now it's not.

It knows my most sober dreams,
and my most drunk dreams,
and all the other dreams in between—
the dreams I dream to occupy
my restless mind with something.

It knows my heart's deepest sorrows.
My insane moments of temporary bliss.
My addictions and habits.

I've written a thousand poems and stories
while smoking on its lap.
It's aware of everything inside my head and heart.
It knows all my embarrassing secrets
and shameful miscalculations.

I feel sorry for it sometimes.
It knows what pain is.
It knows what depression is.
My father watered it with his tears
for many years when his body was filled
with sickness and pain.
When he was wasting away to nothing,
when you could see all his bones.
When he was about to go to the world of the dead.

This bed doesn't only know bugs,
it knows all kinds of other animals too.
Animals more dangerous.
Animals you won't believe exist.
animals that look exactly like me.

It has been burnt a thousand times with cigarette ashes.
It has been peed, vomited, and spat on.

(I don't know about shit,
maybe it has seen it too,
I don't know.)

When I think about it, surely it complains saying:
'Teamhw is always on top of me,
this is no longer love,
it's punishment and abuse.'

If it could push me to the floor,
it would have done so long ago.
And if it wasn't the biggest thing in the room
it would hide and make sure I don't find it.

Why substances?

So we can forget that we are not happy.
Forget that we have dreams that will never come true.
Forget that we are misunderstood.
That the ones we love will never love us,
and will end up in better people's arms.

So that we can forget the good people
who have passed on,
and so we can tolerate the evil ones still alive.
So we can forget the guilt,
the disappointments,
the incurable diseases that eat us,
the dysfunction in our families,
and the parents who never loved us.

So we can forget
that we are hopeless, and helpless.
So we can slow down the speed
of our insecure thoughts.
So we can drown the voices that keep telling us
You won't amount to anything.

Of course we know
reality is pushed away
and death brought closer.
Our intention, however, is to live,
while there's still time—
and to live wholly.

Smoker's dilemma

The whole room smells.
Every piece of furniture,
every piece of clothing.
There is always a cloud inside my room—
though it never rains.

Blue empty packs,
a lighter there,
a matchbox here,
small zip-lock bags,
and 'rolling with the times' sheets.

Even when I am penniless,
the ashtray is always full.

If I can't afford gummed paper,
the grey pages of the KZN telephone directory do,
until only the yellow pages and the cover are left.
And if I run out of the lion's sticks I turn my stove to 6
and wait next to it until it's red.

I smoke more for something to do
than from cravings.
My hands are always itching from the need to be busy,
and so is my brain.

I'm caught in a self-imposed prison.
Chains on my hands, feet, and neck,
lungs, bladder, kidney, stomach and throat.
Chains not visible—
and no one is bothered
whether I escape them or not,
not even I.

Soon I will be handed x-ray scans,
a cancer diagnosed,
and the number of years I have left told to me.

Green

Most mornings I sit with rasta
who is not a real rasta.
The reason he has dreadlocks is to attract clients
and get mind-blowing
discounts from real rastas.
We smoke green for hours on end,
until our brains itch,
then we rub them gently with cigarette smoke.
Rasta likes the tall bong,
I like mine rolled,
and like to smoke it until I am satisfied before I pass it.
I like to think on it until it needs to be lit again.
Rasta is still stuck to the two-pull-vaai routine
famous with school kids and street corner gangs.
That has caused rasta and myself many problems.
But we are One Love now,
that's what he says.
I never agree with him on anything,
except that we never have enough green.

Dream set in heaven

With my two friends.
During a quiet sermon,
one of their hands plays around Christ's
cellphone and platinum watch.
When He starts looking for His things, hysterically,
everyone suggests I should be searched.
God's two bodybuilder angels,
without hesitation, search me.
The stolen items are found,
and other shiny items I didn't know were there.
An assault begins.
An assault worse even than the one received
by Christ back in His day.
I try to run, they catch me.
The assault begins again.
I wake up coughing
and turn on the lights—
it's not blood I was coughing,
just my usual saliva.

Shout out

Shout out to the pickpockets,
the shoplifters,
the housebreakers.

Shout out to the card scammers,
the ATM bombers,
the heist guys,
the fake certificate
and license sellers,
the ganja sellers,
and those who don't need a licence to sell liquor.

Shout out to the guys waiting in the car
for the lights of certain rooms to be turned off,
the guys who are waiting for the security guard to fall asleep.
Those who are always selling something,
those who have it all covered up,
and those who don't care that we know.

Shout out to the guys who did it yesterday
and are now busy looking for a buyer,
the beautiful women who work with the ugliest of men
and play drunk men at bars and hotels,
the stock-stealers in the rural areas and the farms,
the boys who steal and sell the scariest
dogs and cats in the suburbs,
the gamblers who trick their way to victory,
and the guys waiting outside to rob the victors.

Shout out to the person
who is about to do it for the first time,
whose paranoia and chest movements are unbearable.
To the ones who steal anything and everything
and only worry later how they will use or sell it,
the ones who no longer mind being beaten,
who are no longer scared by death.

When it suits me

I admit it,
I've never been fair
to myself or to anyone.

I have told the truth
only when it suited me.
My confessions depended mostly
on how close I was to being caught.
My kindness and loyalty
on what I had to lose.

I used to think of life as a game of cards,
that I had opponents,
and that peeping at their cards
was more important
than carefully studying my own.

I was content with my ignorance,
and saw my stupidity as something to be proud of.
I wore thick black hats and helmets
to block my mind's eye.
There is no crime my mind didn't do,
and no lies my mouth didn't speak.
There were no arrangements I didn't make
to try and escape reality.

Prayer during sleep

Oh my beautiful God—
as your unblinking eyes have seen,
it's decay after decay,
darkness after darkness.
It's sorrow, misery, tears and helplessness.
Thistle after thistle.

Oh gracious God—
please open your ears to my cry—
or at least to the noises in my stomach.
It is a long time that this man has stood in the rain,
without any sign of sunshine—
his umbrella was taken long ago by powerful winds.

Dear God—
enemy of bad actions and thoughts.
The rightful punisher of those who deserve punishment.
The rightful exacting creditor (who doesn't listen to stories
because He says they are all the same).
God who is stern in justice.
Who watches with careful eyes
to discern the errors of men.

Oh owner of heaven—
there is no good this pain
can teach me anymore.
Try to understand my case—
and soften your hand on my throat.

Classroom in Heaven

God the Master has gone out of the classroom.
His Prefect Son is writing down names,
but I am told you can raise a hand.

'May I go out and pee?'
asks one restless student.
'Sit still where you are.'
'But I will burst.'
'Have faith.'

O how I pray my name not to be there
when the Master returns.

III

eShebeen

The big mute bouncer at the door. The boys who play pool whole day and dance to every guitar the jukebox is forced to play. The old man drinking cheap beer by himself in the corner. The always drunk uncle who never needs anyone to dance with. The other uncle who no longer hides the conversations in his head. The new guy who's drunk but tries to look like he's in control. The other drunk guy who touches everyone's girlfriend. The guy who doesn't drink but is always there. The loud energetic guy who talks and laughs across the room. The shy awkward guy who feels guilty for being there. The men in suits at the counter, and the one dead drunk on the toilet floor. The confused intellectual who doesn't stop talking, and the ones next to him who are laughing, hiding their own confusion. The uneducated ones. The young child whose short hands can't reach the counter, but who will be served because they know his mother. The churchgoer who comes every Saturday afternoon to buy church wine. The bar lady who keeps them all buying. The cleaner who knows everything. The dirty guy collecting crates and bottles at the back, who was once the biggest spender in this same bar.

Election manifesto

I will come visit your little shack,
wash your smelly feet,
hold your dirty nose-running shit-smelling children,
buy you a grocery of no importance,
give you t-shirts to wear when you go to town,
push your disabled son's wheelchair
and pretend never to tire.
I will tell my bodyguards
not to push, beat, or shoot you.
I will ask you what you need,
make you touch it, feel it.
But that will be all.
I have a mansion to get back to.
Parties and dates to attend,
and exotic cars to drive—
I am talking a new convertible Porsche Cabriolet,
whose height ends at my hip,
and the latest Range Rover,
bigger than every shack I have seen here.

Leadership

They dress in clothes you never see in stores.
Sleep in hotels you don't know exist.
Eat food you cannot imagine.
When meat is stuck between their teeth,
dentists get involved.
Their wine is so expensive
you can buy a vehicle with just a single bottle.

They are the ones who own the farms
you see on the freeway,
hectares next to hectares.
They also own everything in the cities.
They have interests deep down in the mines
and deep down in the sea.
And interests high up in the sky,
in planes, networks and satellites.
They know where the next road, school, clinic and mall
will be built, and for how much.

The list of monies they deal with
is too long for a cheap calculator.
They buy motor vehicle after motor vehicle,
have houses on top of houses,
with infinite views to the horizon,
swimming pools only a few metres smaller than the ocean.
Their children know nothing of the taste of hardship.

Things remain like this till they die
of serious unknown illnesses
suffered only by gluttons.
The poor love them—
they make them rich.
They wave hands for them at unnecessary meetings,
conferences and rallies,
and sometimes necessary court cases.
They kill each other for them.

Newspapers are full of their scandals,
but people choose to ignore those—
wait, on second thoughts:
maybe I should too.

Lament of a poor man

Times are tough,
stress is high,
children are sick,
there is no food in the house.
At the supermarket my self-esteem is always at its lowest.
It always feels like it's me against the greedy guys,
the greedy business men and women who own the stores,
my greedy boss, the greedy Government
who doesn't regulate this robbery.

What drops my self-esteem
is the prices.
Most of them I cannot believe.
How much is the maize meal?
Sugar?
The brown one too?
Beans?

There is no food in the house.
I am getting way below the minimum wage.
My boss enjoys reminding me
I don't deserve the money he's giving me.
He says he can go to the street
and grab the first non-South African black
and pay him half what he is paying me.
He wants me to hate my fellow brothers, but I won't.
I will just keep working like a slave
and pray he doesn't carry out his threat.

The money I'm getting is too little,
how will I pay the long list of people I have to pay?
How will I get to work till the end of this beginning month?
How will I avoid not borrowing more?
Times are tough,
and the whole roof needs fixing,
rain has ruined all the furniture inside.

Waking up for school

Cold wind making its way through the broken windows.
Rain pouring in from the holes in the corrugated iron roof.
Nongcebo and her group, and the group next to her,
have to move their old shaky desks to the other side.
There are no textbooks.
Only the teacher has them,
and no one knows if she has all of them.
She used to teach Life Orientation,
now she also teaches Maths.
Skhumbuzo's stomach is making noise
and the boys next to him are laughing.
He thinks they are laughing at his shoes.
There are 67 of us in this class.
The school cannot afford other teachers,
they can't afford anything.
It is we who must pay for this – later.

Zim Street, Pietermaritzburg

Again, the sounds start,
'Phumani! Phumani!'
shouts and cries follow,
they are kicking the door,
pointing everyone with rifles—
with real bullets.

Last week they took everything she sells,
the sweets, the chips and biscuits,
the money she had saved in a tin under her bed.

At her door today
they kicked and kicked
until the door was on the floor.
Inside,
just her
and five small starving pair of eyes,
eating from a plate
the size of the youngest's hand.

They do what they came to do,
to kick down doors and send plates flying.
She and the children obey
the kicking
in silence—
not a single word or scream.

When they have left,
she starts again,
fixes the door,
searches for food,
goes back to her trade—
as if they will never come back.

Mqondisi Skhakhane

Mqondisi Skhakhane slept
with a pepper-spray next to his sponge,
and a hatchet, and a taser, and a big dagger under his pillow.
His sleeping shoes were the strong leather
construction safety shoes.
Laces tightly fastened—
not even a smell could get out.
He slept with a helmet on.
Locked his room with two locks.
He was tired of dreams fucking him up.
During the day,
he had two pistols on his waist
(a third one in his side bag),
and a Rambo pocket knife in his pocket.
After a short conversation with him,
he had to search you—
Unashamedly he would ask you
to put your hands up and separate your legs.
He always stayed sober,
and always looked over his shoulder.
He was tired of reality fucking him up.
He was tired of everything.
And who could blame him?
His side of the story was never known.

Always Petros Mwelase

A never complaining heart.
No anger for him.
No revenge.
Unshaken by compliments,
criticism meant nothing either.

Big hands, dirty from clean work
or clean waiting to lift someone up.
Others always came first—
even if sleep made them late.

Always calm, ready for a laugh.
Always ready to give an ear.
Always Petros Mwelase.
Always.

I want to build you a house

for Elana Bregin

i want to build you a (firm) house, on a (solid) rock,
at the centre of an (unknown and unknowable) future.
a room for your carefulness, and attentiveness,
for your thoughtfulness and stimulating wit,
for your kindness, boundless care, and receptiveness.

(O how i wish i could add more rooms for
the dogs and wild things you so dearly love—
but human laws will never allow it,
not even in the future).

the stones have been gathered,
the cement bought, and tools borrowed.
i have a smile on my face.
i have a plan—
and your unfailing words as its guide.

Mabhece my mother's mother

RIP Bancamile Generoza Khubone (1946–2020)

Grown old,
her pale skin could no longer take in a whole day's sunshine,
nor stand half a minute of cold rain.
Her eyes could no longer see as they used to,
but could see what she wanted them to see.
Her ears couldn't hear,
could no longer take in the fast music
she used to move so beautifully to.
Her throat and liver could no longer take in
the spirits they were so familiar with.
She now only drank with her eyes
and her imagination.
Her feet, knees, hips – all grown stiff,
the dances she used to excel at could no longer be performed.
Everything could now only be done with just the eyes—
she sat and stared.

IV

The greatest sin

There is no sin greater
than not having money.
You don't need go to hell
to be punished for it.
You get punished for it here on Earth.
Severely.
And you never get a chance to explain.

Early morning

I have searched for a cigarette everywhere.
I did not find one.
I slept with the key hanging in the lock from outside.
But that's not what bothers me.
What bothers me is that I haven't found a cigarette.

Thinking, calculating.
Calculating, thinking.
As I have nothing to think about,
my head turns to thinking about anything and everything—
the people who said they will catch me
and slit my throat,
the difficulties I underestimated,
and all the time I spent on illusions.

I fight a war like this most nights.
I know the battlefield better
than I know anything.
In the morning
time takes its own time
before it makes things clear,
and I always ask myself,
why does the sun have to rise,
why doesn't it leave us alone in the dark.

It was poetry

When I started school I could write my name – Surname –
And I could draw a cat – In grade one teachers gave me poems
to read and recite in front of visiting teachers – Though I
couldn't read the English written inside – I wouldn't play
with anything else but books – In grade three my sister and I
used my father's desk as our office desk where a lot of our first
writings were done – Grade six I read A Rock and a Hard Place:
One Boy's Triumphant Story – The book about a small boy
who got AIDS from his parents' drinking friends – I wasn't the
same after – One of my stepsisters forgot her diary before she
left for work – I didn't go to school that day – Her eyes were
closed – Everyone's eyes were closed – Only I saw poetry – The
end of that same year – I walked from Pietermaritzburg CBD
to eMkhondeni – Shuter and Shooter publishers – fifteen
kilometres there and back – With hundreds of hand-written
pages – Topics like – AIDS – Being rejected – And triumphing
over it – A senior employee called by the receptionist took the
stack out of my hands and read it for few a seconds – turned
some pages and read for a few more seconds – He gave me my
stack back – Put his hand on my shoulder – Smiled – 'You think
too much' – 'Go play with other kids son and enjoy yourself'–
'You are still young!' – He continued to smile – Turned around
and left – Before he entered the big door that led to many
other offices he shouted – 'Don't stop writing though!' – Grade
seven – Mrs Chetty – Senior librarian at Bessie Head Library
in Pietermaritzburg – Miraculously – Selected for me the kind
of books that would get me hooked on reading forever and
nothing else – I quit everything – I couldn't wait to see her at
the end of every week – Grade nine – She looked at my library
card through her eyeglasses which were always at the tip of her
nose and says Bessie too was born in Pietermaritzburg – On
my birthday – The sixth of July – I searched deeper – Bessie's

mother passed away when she was six – My mother passed
away when I was six too – Grade ten – Mrs Laljeeth tells me
I shouldn't do anything except write – I read my pieces to my
uninterested friends every morning – Every single morning
– Grade eleven – I read Antonije Isaković's 'April Fool's Day' –
Life changed completely – I was certain – However – Two years
later my father looked me straight in the eyes and asked me
what I want to do with my future – My head and heart screamed
Poetry – But my mouth slowly said Law – He smiled – Opened
his wallet and gave me bus fare to go ask what was needed
– He was sick – I couldn't say anything else – I put my head
down – Four years – Doing less reading – Writing only a few
poems – When it was time to find a job – However – I locked
myself in my room and chose to read and write as I wanted –
When I wanted – Even though I starved – No one could tell
me anything – My father who could have told me something
was dead – It went on for years – I couldn't be stopped – I met
a brilliant writer – Forced a correspondence – It didn't work – I
was suicidal – I lost my mind – Found it again – Lost it again
– And one night – Miraculously – I met an old man – Who
rescued me – Told me – And showed me – That things will be
fine – That there was no need to throw in the towel – O how I
thank God repeatedly for that man – Simple though it sounds –
That was poetry – The sweetest and rawest my ears ever tasted.

To my beautiful ex

You call my writings a waste of time.
You tell me nothing goes or comes
anymore in my life.
That I have reduced my life
to staring at old papers
written by old bitter dead men.

You say you don't understand
why I'm not like other men.
Why I don't chase fame, money, acclaim
or your friends.

You say if my pens and papers were alcohol
I wouldn't by now have a liver or a face.
And if they were real work
we wouldn't have all these complications.

You always shout and say
Go and find a real job
and work like other men!
But you seem not to see
that you are disturbing me
while I am really working.

Telling the pages

I rush home to tell the pages
my love has been rejected again.
I get no motivation.
No pat on the back.
No counsel.
Just a blank look staring straight into my red watery eyes.
I try to speak louder but it doesn't help.

O dear God,
what am I to be
if even the pages reject me?

My dirty room

To the ants that feed on my mistakes when I eat,
the fast spiders that I always miss when I try to kill,
the lizards that hide behind my father's photographs,
and my always incorrect wall clock.
To the attention-seeking bugs
I share my mattress and pillows with,
the flies in the kitchen,
the big mosquitoes the size of a bird,
the thousand cockroaches
that wait for the lights to be turned off,
the rats that play with my mind
and leave me seeing things that are not there,
the fat snake under the sink, and its snakelets.
I see myself in all of you,
hope you see yourselves in me too.
We are in all this together.
This poem is for you.

Death is on his way

Like a loan-shark, he is coming.
No type of lock will deny him entry.
You will regret that you never
gave him the attention he deserves.

You won't believe
that all along he was fooling you,
putting you in a false sense of security
so you did everything recklessly.
You won't believe that none of it
was ever free—
though nothing was ever enough.

You will beg,
weep at his feet, make promises,
admit your mistakes, ask for forgiveness.
But soon you will realise you are talking to yourself.

You will then call him names,
show your anger and frown with your whole face.
But he won't be disturbed.
He will just stand there
and give you his empty hand.

And if you have wasted your time,
know he won't waste his.

News about His passing

God has died.
His funeral will be in few days' time.
Though the burial place is unknown,
attendance is compulsory.
Absence will be a serious offence.

I heard the Man had no friends,
but one can be assured everyone knew Him.
They say death, His own creation, sadly turned against Him.
That He overdosed on His own medicine.
Some say guilt caused Him a heart attack,
some say He slashed His big balls and set them alight,
others say He starved Himself to death.

Some are still disputing His death,
and say they will only believe
when they see His casket
and have thrown dust in His chest or face.
I say Rest in Peace old man,
again, you took us by surprise.

Printed in the United States
by Baker & Taylor Publisher Services